DATE DUE

SEP 29		
JA 5 '99		
APR 29		

Demco

Holidays & Festivals

SIKH FESTIVALS

Dr. Sukhbir Singh Kapoor

Rourke Enterprises, Inc.
Vero Beach, Florida 32964

Holidays and Festivals

Buddhist Festivals
Christmas
Easter
Halloween
Hindu Festivals

Jewish Festivals
Muslim Festivals
New Year
Sikh Festivals
Thanksgiving and Harvest

Test © 1989 Rourke Enterprises, Inc.
PO Box 3328, Vero Beach, Florida 32964

This book is dedicated to my beloved son, Prince. My thanks are due to Preetbir, Alka, Tracy and Ramanbir Singh Kapoor for their valuable suggestions.

Library of Congress Cataloging-in-Publication Data

Kapoor, Sukhbir Singh.
    Sikh festivals / Sukhbir Singh Kapoor.
        p.   cm. – (Holidays & festivals)
    Bibliography: p.
    Summary: Describes the origins and traditions of Sikh festivals and celebrations around the world.
    ISBN 0-86592-984-X
    1.Fasts and feasts–Sikhism–Juvenile literature.   2. Sikhism–Customs and practices–Juvenile literature. [1. Fasts and feasts–Sikhism 2. Sikhism–Customs and practices.] 1. Title.   11. Series: Holidays and festivals.
    BL2018.37.K37 1989
    249.6'36–dc19   88–15717
                                                          CIP
                                                          AC

Printed in Italy by Tipolitografia G. Canale & C. S.p.A. - Turin

Contents

Celebrating Sikh Festivals

Sikhs around the World

There are more than sixteen million Sikhs. Most live in the Punjab, an area of northwest India and Pakistan, which is where the Sikh religion was born. There are also Sikhs in other parts of India, East Africa, Britain, the United States, Canada, Iran, Afghanistan, Malaysia, Singapore, the Philippines, Australia and New Zealand. There are about a quarter of a million Sikhs in Britain, making the largest Sikh community outside India. Less than 10,000 Sikhs live in North America.

Sikhs believe in God and living according to God's will. Family life, honesty, hard work and helping other people in the community are important parts of their religion. Sikhs must not smoke, drink alcohol or use non-medical drugs. The Sikh religion is based on the teachings of prophets called Gurus. Guru is an Indian word meaning religious teacher. Sikhism was founded by Guru Nanak in the fifteenth century, and his teachings were carried on by nine other Gurus over the next two hundred years.

Every year, there are various festivals to celebrate the anniversaries of the Gurus. These are called *gurpurbs*. Other festivals are called *melas* (fairs). Sikhs celebrate their festivals by the

A young Sikh bride, dressed in a traditional red wedding sari.

Two boys, dressed to represent the sons of Guru Gobind Singh, take part in a festival procession.

lunar calendar, which is based on the movements of the moon. A month is measured as the time between two new moons. This means that the date of a festival is not the same every year. There is only one festival –*Baisakhi* – that is on a fixed date every year. In Western countries it is difficult to celebrate a festival on a working day, so the nearest Sunday to the date is chosen.

The *Gurdwara*

A Sikh church, or temple, is called a *gurdwara*. *Gurdwara* is a Punjabi word that means "House of God." Besides being a place of worship, a *gurdwara* is also a community center where social activities, advice sessions and educational classes on Sikhism may be held. It has a kitchen and a dining room.

The *gurdwara* has a prayer hall where services are held. At one end of the room, the Sikh Holy Book, the Guru Granth Sahib, is kept on a platform covered with a richly decorated canopy. Behind it sits the *granthi,* or reader. People sit on the floor during the service, men on the right and women and children on the left. Sikhs take off their shoes before entering the prayer hall and cover their heads as a mark of respect.

The service is conducted in Punjabi. There are prayers, hymns, readings and sermons, lasting

Preparing a meal in the gurdwara kitchen. Everybody eats together after a service.

6

for about two hours. The Guru Granth Sahib is written in a script called *Gurmukhi,* a word meaning "from the mouth of the Guru." Sikh children who have been brought up outside India often go to special classes at the *gurdwara* to learn *Gurmukhi*

Most Sikh men who live in North America or Europe wear Western clothes to their jobs, but sometimes they wear Indian clothes to go to the *gurdwara.* These are usually *churidar pajamas* and a *kurta* (tight-fitting trousers and a loose shirt). All strict Sikh men wear a turban. Sikh women may wear *salwar-kameez* (tunic and trousers) or a dress called a *sari.* A long scarf called a *dupatta* or a *chuni* is worn over the head and around the shoulders. Many younger Sikhs and children wear Western clothes all the time.

A service in the gurdwara's *prayer hall.*

Gurpurbs

The main *gurpurbs* are Guru Nanak's birthday, Guru Arjan's martyrdom, Guru Tegh Bahadur's martyrdom, Guru Gobind Singh's birthday and the celebration of the Sikhs' Holy Book. In India, many hundreds of thousands of people join in the celebrations, and colorful processions parade through the streets. Outside India, celebrations are held only in the *gurdwara*.

A special service is held at the *gurdwara* on a *gurpurb*. Two days before the *gurpurb*, an *Akhand Path*, which is a continuous reading of the Guru Granth Sahib, is held in every *gurdwara* and house that has its own Holy Book. Relays of men and women spend one or two hours reading. Normally it takes a minimum of forty-eight hours to finish the entire book. The reading is concluded on the morning of the *gurpurb*, and as many Sikhs as possible try to come to listen to

Ragis – *musicians – sing a hymn during a service.*

the final pages. The service starts after this, at about 5 a.m., with the singing of *Asa-di-var*, a hymn composed by Guru Nanak.

Listening to a reading from the Guru Granth Sahib.

This is followed by other hymns, or *kirtan*, from the Guru Granth Sahib. These are often accompanied by musical instruments. Then there are prayers, readings, discussions, lectures on Sikh life and history, and sermons. These are all related to the life of the Guru whose festival is being celebrated. The *Ardas* prayer (a special set prayer at the end of the service) is followed by the distribution of the sacrament, *karah parshad*, to the congregation. *Karah parshad* is made from semolina, butter and sugar.

After the service, which lasts all morning, everyone goes to the dining room for a meal. The meal, and the kitchen where it is prepared, are called *langar*. Both *langar* and *karah parshad* symbolize unity and equality among Sikhs.

9

The Birthday of Guru Nanak

The Founder of Sikhism

Guru Nanak was the founder of the Sikh religion. He was born in November 1469, and Sikhs celebrate his birthday every year. This is the most important of the Sikh *gurpurbs*. As Christians celebrate the birth of Jesus Christ, so Sikhs celebrate the birth of Guru Nanak. The festival usually lasts for three days. During this time every Sikh family visits their *gurdwara*.

Guru Nanak was born in a small village about 41 miles (65 kilometers) from Lahore, which is now in Pakistan. Legends say that at the time of his birth, the heavens showered flowers on the earth, and musical instruments started playing on their own. The main religions followed in

Guru Nanak's meeting with God, when he was told he was to be a prophet.

India at that time were Hinduism and Islam. Although born a Hindu, Guru Nanak disagreed with much of the Hindu way of life.

According to Sikh legend, in November 1496 Guru Nanak was taken to God by the angels. He stayed in God's presence for three days, and God told him that he was to be his prophet. Guru Nanak's absence from the village led to rumors that he had drowned in a local stream, where he had last been seen bathing. But Guru Nanak reappeared and set off on a lifetime's mission to spread the message of God. Guru Nanak is one of the most traveled prophets in history. He went to Tibet, Ceylon (now Sri Lanka), Bangladesh and Mecca. Guru Nanak's teachings, in the form of poems and hymns, are preserved in the Sikh Holy Book – the Guru Granth Sahib. He wanted to unite Hindus and Muslims with a religion devoted to the will of God, love, truth and equality. The people who followed Guru Nanak

Guru Nanak traveled widely, spreading the word of God. Here he is shown with two followers, Bala and Mardana, on the back of a fish.

became known as Sikhs, from the Sanskrit word meaning disciple.

In the last days of his life, Guru Nanak lived in a village called Kartarpur. When he was dying there was a quarrel among his followers. His Hindu followers wanted to cremate him, whereas his Muslim followers wanted to bury him. The next day, his followers found that the body had gone. Guru Nanak wanted to show that the way of God was neither Hindu nor Muslim, yet it included both.

Guru Nanak was succeeded by nine other Gurus who carried on his work. Sikhs believe that although the ten prophets were different people, they all had the same spirit.

Sikhs representing the Panj Pyare, *the first baptized Sikhs, lead a procession. The Guru Granth Sahib is carried on a covered litter.*

A procession ends outside a gurdwara.

In India, there is usually a procession the day before the birthday of Guru Nanak. It is led by the *Panj Pyare* (any five baptized Sikhs, representing the first baptized Sikhs – the *Khalsa*). They hold ceremonial swords and carry the Guru Granth Sahib on a covered litter. Following them are groups of schoolchildren, scouts, students, men and women, all singing hymns. The procession normally passes through the streets and ends outside the central *gurdwara*. Streets are often covered with bunting and other decorations. Free food, drinks and sweets are served along the route.

In Britain, the celebrations are a mixture of religious occasion, social gathering and fun for children. Special events are arranged such as fairs, games and fêtes. There are stalls offering a variety of foods and sweets.

The Martyrdom of Guru Arjan

The First Sikh Martyr

Guru Arjan was the fifth Guru and the first Sikh martyr. He was tortured to death on the orders of Emperor Jehangir. The anniversary of his martyrdom falls in the month of May or June. Sikhs celebrate it with the same sadness as Christians feel at Easter.

There are ten Sikh Gurus. At first the guruship could not be passed on by a Guru to his son. But after the time of the fourth Guru, Ram Das, the guruship remained in the families of his descendants. Guru Arjan was the youngest son of Guru Ram Das. He had two older brothers, but Guru Ram Das found Arjan to be the most

The Golden Temple at Amritsar was built by Guru Arjan.

worthy of the guruship. He was eighteen years old when his father died, and he was appointed the fifth Guru in 1581.

Guru Arjan was a man of devotion, simplicity and humility. He remained the Guru for twenty-five years. In this period he accomplished a great many tasks. In the new city of Amritsar, which had been founded by his father, Guru Arjan built a large temple for Sikhs to worship in, called *Harimandir* (Abode of the Lord). This temple is popularly known as the Golden Temple. It was built with four doors, one at each side, as a way of saying that the temple was open to men and women of all castes and from the four corners of the earth.

Guru Arjan was also responsible for collecting the first version of the Sikh scriptures. He added

Many Sikhs were tortured by the Mogul rulers. Here, a martyr is cooked to death.

some hymns of his own and other Gurus to the collected teachings of Guru Nanak, and also included some works by Hindus and Muslims who had similar beliefs to Sikhs. This was called *Adi Granth* (the First Collection).

There were a lot of conversions to the Sikh faith during the time of Guru Arjan. This was very unpopular with the Muslim rulers. Emperor Jehangir ordered the arrest of Guru Arjan. After a fake trial, Guru Arjan was sentenced to death by torture. He was made to sit on a burning-hot plate, then he was boiled alive and hot sand was poured over his body. He died in May 1606.

Like Jesus, Guru Arjan's only crime was that he was preaching God's message. He challenged the corrupt practices of the rulers and the rituals of the existing religions.

A Sikh boys' band marches in a procession to celebrate the martyrdom of Guru Arjan.

16

The anniversary of Guru Arjan's martyrdom is celebrated in a similar way to the birthday of Guru Nanak. Families visit the *gurdwara* for the special service that is held on a *gurpurb*, and other events are organized to mark the occasion.

In India there are processions, and in the Punjab people arrange the distribution of free drinks on every road. May, the month Guru Arjan died, is one of the hottest months in India, with a temperature of about 120°F (49°C). During his torture, Guru Arjan was not allowed to drink any water. As a sign of respect, Sikhs offer free drinks on the day of his martyrdom to every passerby, to remind them of the sufferings of the Guru and the cause he died for.

Selling festival garlands in Amritsar.

The Martyrdom of Guru Tegh Bahadur

A Sacrifice for Others

Guru Tegh Bahadur was the ninth Guru and second Sikh martyr. The anniversary of his martyrdom is in November or December. Guru Tegh Bahadur gave his life to save Hindus. It was a sacrifice for a religion other that his own, and Sikhs feel proud to celebrate it, for the Guru taught them a lesson:

Most people live for themselves
Very few live for others. . .

A Sikh soldier buys a picture of Guru Gobind Singh, from a stall selling portraits of the Gurus at the festival of Guru Tegh Bahadur.

Guru Tegh Bahadur was born in Amritsar in April 1621. He became the Guru at the age of forty-three. A cruel Mogul Emperor named Aurangzeb ruled India at that time. He was a tyrant and decided to convert all the people of India to Islam. He ordered that all those who refused to become Muslims were to be killed. Most people in India were Hindus, and every day many thousands of them were converted to Islam, either by threats or bribes.

People were desperate. A delegation of Hindu priests (representing the Hindu community) called on Guru Tegh Bahadur at Anandpur for help and advice. They talked for many hours. Eventually a decision was made. The priests would tell Aurangzeb that if he could convert

Sikhs always wash before entering a gurdwara. *These people have made a pilgrimage to a* gurdwara *dedicated to Guru Tegh Bahadur.*

Guru Tegh Bahadur to Islam, then the whole Hindu community would become Muslims without any further resistance.

This was a very big challenge for Aurangzeb. He summoned the Guru to Delhi, the capital of India. The Guru reached Delhi with his five disciples and they were all arrested and presented to the Emperor. All sorts of concessions, rewards and bribes were offered to the Guru if he converted to Islam, but he refused them all. As a last resort the Emperor threatened torture. To frighten the Guru into changing his mind, all his disciples were tortured to death before his eyes. One was tied between two posts and sawed in half; one was tied up and thrown into a cauldron of boiling oil; another was hacked to pieces limb by limb. The other two disciples were also subjected to terrible tortures. Despite these horrors, the Guru still refused to change his religion and was beheaded. This sad incident happened in November 1675.

Guru Tegh Bahadur gave his life but probably saved the whole Hindu population from annihilation. He also upheld the honor and bravery of the Sikh people.

Guru Tegh Bahadur's martyrdom taught Sikhs a new lesson: sacrifice yourself for the good of others. The festival in his memory is celebrated mainly in Delhi and at *gurdwaras* dedicated to Guru Tegh Bahadur. There are processions, and pictures of atrocities that took place during the time of the Mogul rulers are displayed along the route. Posters of the Hindu priests sitting in the presence of the Guru and discussing their problems with him are also shown. At the place

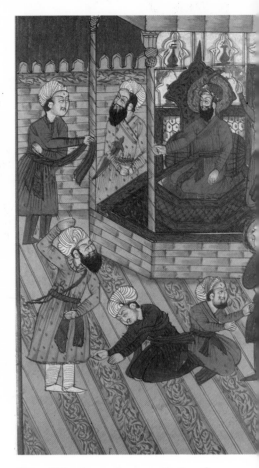

The Hindu priests ask for Guru Tegh Bahadur's help to fight persecution by the Moguls.

in Delhi where the Guru was beheaded, the Sikhs have built a very large temple known as the *Gurdwara Sisganj*. This shrine is the focal point for the celebrations of the festival.

The banner in the procession depicts that Guru Tegh Bahadur saved the Hindu religion.

The Birthday of Guru Gobind Singh

The Last Guru

Guru Gobind Singh was the tenth and last Guru. He was born in December 1666. His birthday celebrations are in December or January. After Guru Nanak's birthday, this is the most important *gurpurb*. Guru Gobind Singh founded the *Khalsa* and declared that the Granth Sahib, the Holy Book, should be the "Guru" after him.

Guru Gobind Singh's two young sons were buried alive when they refused to become Muslims.

Eating langar *on Guru Gobind Singh's birthday. In Britain, the food is often served on stainless steel plates like these.*

Guru Gobind Singh was born in Patna, where he lived for five years before his family moved to the Punjab. He was brought up like a prince, learning many languages and receiving religious and military instruction.

He said, in one of his hymns, that he had been sent by God to this world with a special mission.

Gobind Singh became the Guru after his father, Guru Tegh Bahadur, was executed in Delhi. The Mogul rulers were cruel tyrants, who would not allow any faith except Islam to be practiced. Anybody who had other beliefs was persecuted. Guru Gobind Singh wanted Sikhs to be strong enough to defend their religion. On the festival of *Baisakhi* in 1699, he called all his followers together and created the *Khalsa* (see pages 31-32) – a religious brotherhood united in its determination to defend Sikhism.

The Guru suffered at the hands of emperors and people of other faiths. He sacrificed his four sons for the causes of humanity and justice. Two of his sons were buried alive by the administrators of Sirhand, a town in the Punjab, when they refused to convert to Islam. They were only five and eight years old. The other two sons, aged fourteen and eighteen, died heroic deaths in a battle with the Moguls at Chamkaur, another town in the Punjab. The Guru had lost his own father when he was only nine years old.

Guru Gobind Singh's message to the world was friendship, love, humanity and humility. He said that Sikhs should pray every day, help the needy,

Distributing langar *in the grounds of a* gurdwara *in New Delhi, during the birthday celebrations. In India the food is often served in leaves.*

and make sacrifices for others. He taught that there was only one God, forbade the worship of images, and condemned all religious rituals since God's word could only be realized by love and truthful living. He believed in equality between men and women.

He died in Nanded, a town in the south of India. A beautiful shrine known as *Takht Hazur Sahib* has been built there.

Guru Gobind Singh taught Sikhs to make sacrifices for others.

All over the world Sikhs celebrate this *gurpurb.* In addition to the religious celebrations, games and sports competitions are organized for this festival. People often make pilgrimages to visit the *Takht Patna Sahib* (a shrine where the Guru was born), the *Takht Hazur Sahib* and the Golden Temple at Amritsar.

The Sikh Holy Book

The Guru Granth Sahib

Three days before Guru Gobind Singh died, he called his followers together and told them that after his death there would be no more human Gurus. In future, the Granth Sahib would be the Sikhs' Guru. Guru Gobind Singh made this announcement in October 1708. Sikhs celebrate its anniversary in September or October.

Every day, Sikhs say a prayer:

Believe in Guru Granth
It is the body and soul of the Guru
Those who want to find God
Can find Him in the hymns written in the Granth.

The second Guru, Angad, had collected together all the hymns of Guru Nanak. Arjan (the fifth Guru) added other hymns and teachings to these, making the *Adi Granth* (the First Collection). Guru Gobind Singh made the final additions to the collection. The Guru Granth Sahib is 1,430 pages long.

Guru Gobind Singh was the last Guru. He realized that God's message had been conveyed to the people, and that the mission of the Guru had been completed. He called a gathering of his followers and placed a volume of the Holy Book before the congregation. Then he placed

All strict Sikhs wear five symbols of the faith – unshorn hair, a comb, a steel bracelet, shorts and a sword. These are known as the five Ks.

five coins and a coconut in front of the Holy Book and bowed before it, declaring that from that moment onward, the Granth was to be the spiritual teacher of the Sikhs.

Sikhs treat the Guru Granth Sahib with greater reverence than, for example, the Christians show for the Bible. This is because the Guru Granth Sahib is not only a religious document but it also enjoys the status of a Guru. Sikhs only worship God. They do not worship their Gurus and do not worship the Guru Granth Sahib.

An Akhand Path, *a continuous reading of the Guru Granth Sahib.*

27

The Guru Granth Sahib is kept on a platform under a richly decorated canopy, or covered with a special cloth. Both are a sign of respect. Sikhs must always bow before the Guru Granth Sahib when they enter the prayer hall, and must never turn their backs to it. Most people place an offering of food or money in front of it. Food is used for *langar*. A *chaur* is kept next to the Guru Granth Sahib. This is similar to a fly whisk, or brush, and is waved over the Holy Book as a sign of respect. All those who read the Guru Granth

A Sikh wedding takes place before the Guru Granth Sahib.

Sahib must wash their hands before touching it.

The celebrations of the anniversary of the Guru Granth Sahib are all religious, with a special service at the *gurdwara*. Afterward, everyone eats *langar* together.

Cooking chapatties *in the kitchen of the Golden Temple, Amritsar. These will be eaten for* langar *after the service.*

Baisakhi

Baisakhi is the first day of the Sikh and Hindu New Year. It is celebrated on April 13. In the Punjab it marks the end of the spring wheat harvest festival. All over the world, Sikhs go to their *gurdwaras* to remember the creation of the *Khalsa* by Guru Gobind Singh.

Guru Gobind Singh wanted to make the Sikhs' faith so strong that they would never denounce it in times of trouble. He called all his followers to attend a conference. It was held on April 13, 1699 at Anandpur, a small town in the Punjab.

A gurdwara at Anandpur, the town where Guru Gobind Singh formed the Khalsa on Baisakhi 1699.

During the conference the Guru called for a volunteer who was prepared to give his life for the faith, to show his dedication to God.

A man named Daya Ram rose and said he would do so. Guru Gobind Singh took him into a tent. After a few minutes the Guru appeared with a bloodstained sword and called for four more volunteers. Most of the people were terrified, but four men came forward. They too were taken inside the tent.

Everyone thought the five men had been killed, but later they reappeared alive, dressed in shining yellow clothes and decorated with weapons. In front of the whole congregation the Guru baptized them with *amrit*. The Guru called the men *Panj Pyare* (five beloved Sikhs) and asked them to use the word *singh* (lion) as their surname. He named the group *Khalsa* (the pure ones) and ordered them to maintain five

During the time of the Gurus, there was much fighting between the Sikhs and Moguls.

symbols of the faith: unshorn hair, a comb, a steel bracelet, shorts worn as underwear and a sword.

Since that time, all strict Sikhs have worn the five symbols, commonly called the five Ks. Men wear a turban to keep their hair tidy. Before putting on the turban, the hair is tied with a piece of cloth called a *patka*. Boys may just wear a *patka* until they are old enough to wear a turban. Male Sikhs take the name Singh as part of their surname when they are baptized, and females take the name Kaur (meaning princess).

Baisakhi is often a time when Sikhs are initiated, or baptized. The ceremony is called *Asmrit Chhakna* and is conducted by the *Panj Pyare*, five Sikhs who are already baptized. The person being initiated drinks *amrit*, the baptismal water, which is prepared by the *Panj Pyare. Amrit* is made from sugar and water, which are stirred together with a double-edged sword, while five *banis* (daily prayers) are read.

On Baisakhi, *the Sikh flag is hoisted outside the* gurdwara *to mark the New Year.*

32

Celebrating *Baisakhi*

In the morning, all families visit the nearest *gurdwara* to pray. There are events taking place at the *gurdwara* all day. From early in the morning until lunch-time, there are hymns, speeches and prayers. The people then gather in the *gurdwara's* dining hall for a community lunch. During the early evening, people recite poetry to emphasize the importance of the *Khalsa*. This is followed by prayers and dinner.

Later in the evening, there are social gatherings in the local communities, with singing and dancing. The highlights of the occasion are two dances – the *Bhangra* dance by the men, and the *Giddha* dance by the women.

Colorful Sikh dancers perform Bhangra *at social events*.

Diwali

The Festival of Light

Diwali is a festival of light. It is both a seasonal and a religious festival, which takes place in October or November. Sikhs remember the release of Guru Hargobind from prison.

Hindus also celebrated *Diwali* as a festival of light. Several of their legends are associated with it. Jains (the followers of Jainism, another Indian religion) mark *Diwali* as the day their prophet Mahavir received the word of God.

Sparklers and fireworks are popular at Diwali.

Hargobind, who was to become the sixth Guru, was born in June 1595. When he was eleven years old, his father, Guru Arjan (the fifth Guru), was tortured to death by the Moguls. Guru Hargobind became a powerful leader. Jehangir, the Mogul Emperor, was scared of the Guru's power and popularity, and resented the fact that many Muslims were being converted to the Sikh faith. He had the Guru arrested and imprisoned. Guru Hargobind was kept in a fort at Gwalior for two years, for not paying a fine that had been inflicted on his father, and for allegedly plotting against the Moguls.

When he was released, the Guru returned to Amritsar. The Sikh community lit every house

Diwali celebrates Guru Hargobind's release from prison. This picture shows him hunting a tiger.

with candles as a sign of celebration, and ever since that time Sikhs have celebrated Diwali with lights and fireworks.

Celebrating *Diwali*

Diwali marks the end of the very hot summer in India and the start of the winter season, when winter crops will be sown. People decorate their houses with lights: in the villages, special pots are made from clay to form lamps (known as *divas*); in the cities and in Western countries, lights and candles may be used instead. In Amritsar, the Golden Temple is illuminated by hundreds of small lights, which are hung in strings around the building.

The festival is celebrated over five days, of which the third day is *Diwali* proper. People give

Schoolchildren acting out one of the Diwali *legends in a play.*

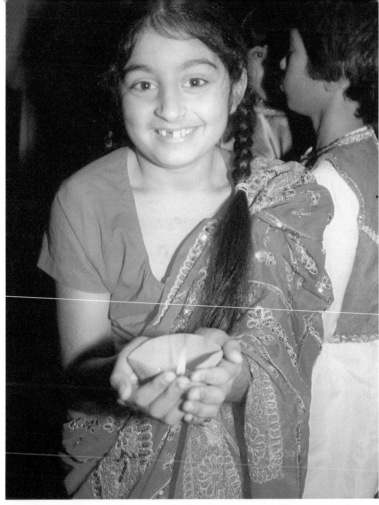

Small lamps called divas *are lit at* Diwali.

each other boxes of Indian candies, such as *Burfi, Laddoo, Gulab Jaman, Rasgoolas,* and other presents. People dress up in new clothes and there is music and dancing, making *Diwali* a very colorful festival.

Like Christmas, *Diwali* is also a family occasion. In the evening, all the houses are decorated with candles or *divas,* and there are firework parties. At dinner-time the whole family gathers to eat together. Sikhs visit *gurdwaras* in the evening to pray, whereas Hindus prefer to pray at home. Late at night, older members of the family may sit down to play cards, perhaps continuing until dawn the next day.

Hola Mohalla

The Story of *Hola Mohalla*

Hola Mohalla is celebrated in February or March. This is spring in India and the fields bloom with beautiful and colorful flowers.

The festival of *Hola Mohalla* has its roots in the Hindu festival of *Holi*. At *Holi*, Hindus celebrate a popular legend: the escape of Prahlad, King Hirayakashipu's son, from the goddess Holika. People have a lot of fun at this time, but celebrations may become rather boisterous!

Distributing karah parshad *after the service in the* gurdwara *on* Hola Mohalla.

Guru Gobind Singh (the tenth Guru) introduced *Hola Mohalla* in 1680. He disapproved of Sikhs taking part in the Hindu festival and decided to provide an alternative event. He organized a gathering at Anandpur, calling it *Hola Mohalla*. Guru Gobind Singh decided this would be a good occasion to train his army by performing mock battles and military exercises. This was done before the whole Sikh community.

Besides the military events, there were also sports, music and poetry competitions.

Both Sikhs and Hindus may join in together with sports competitions at Hola Mohalla.

Celebrations

Hola Mohalla is an occasion when Sikhs enjoy organizing sports such as horseback riding and athletics. People may shower each other with colored water called *gulal,* using sprinklers specially made for the festival.

The main place where *Hola Mohalla* is celebrated is at Anandpur, the town in India where Guru Gobind Singh held the first *Hola Mohalla*. There is a three-day fair where crowds assemble in large numbers to witness a variety of sports activities and processions.

At places outside the Punjab and especially in the West, the celebrations are similar to those in Anandpur. Many games and tournaments are organized by various Sikh institutions. On the last day, the people go to *gurdwaras* and pray to be kept healthy and strong.

A kabadi tournament. This is a special Sikh game.

Other Melas

Basant

Basant is a spring festival, celebrated by Sikhs and Hindus in the month of January or February. People make a point of wearing something yellow, because it is a spring color. Men wear *Many families cook yellow rice to eat on* Basant.

yellow turbans and the women wear yellow *saris* or *salwar-kameez* (tunic and trousers) with a yellow *chuni* (scarf).

Basant is a time for families to get together. In villages and in many towns in India, kite-flying competitions are held. The main meals of the day are made with yellow rice specially cooked for the occasion.

Many youngsters have started to celebrate *Basant* the same way we celebrate St. Valentine's Day. Couples in love make this a special day of the year. *Basant* is also considered to be a holy day for young children to start school, which they normally do at the age of five.

Children in India, like these British children, start school at the age of five. Sikhs consider Basant *to be a holy day to start school.*

Maghi

This festival is celebrated every year in January. When Guru Gobind Singh was besieged by the Mogul army at Anandpur, forty of his very close followers deserted him. When these deserters reached home, the women would not let them into the houses. They were angry because the men had betrayed the Guru. One of the women, Mai Bhago, then spoke to the men about the importance of dying for the cause.

The men were sorry for their action, and under the command of Mai Bhago, they returned to the Guru. Together they fought and defeated the Moguls at the Battle of Muktsar. But the men were killed, giving their lives for the Guru and for justice. There is a big festival every year at Muktsar.

Guru Gobind Singh tears up the letter of desertion from his forty followers, after they returned to fight and die for him at the Battle of Muktsar.

Lohri

Lohri is celebrated in January, to mark the end of winter in India. It is also a festival devoted to young women, who pray to God that they will make a good marriage. At *Lohri,* young girls and boys go from home to home to collect money for the night-time celebrations.

The story of this festival dates back to the sixteenth century. In a village called Sandalbar lived a man named Dulla Bhutti, who arranged marriages.

As children go from home to home collecting money at *Lohri,* they sing poems known as *vars,* which are addressed to Dulla Bhutti.

Lohri is a night festival. Huge bonfires are lit and the young women dance around them. Candies called *reuori* and *chirwara* are eaten and thrown at the fire. Sikhs who have recently had a birth in the family celebrate *Lohri* with a feast.

Rakhsha Bandhan

This is also known as *Rakhi.* The festival is Hindu in origin, but is celebrated by all Indians. A sister ties a *rakhi* (a ribbon) around her brother's arm, and the brother vows to defend her honor all his life. The sister normally gives her brother a box of candies, and the brother normally gives her some money in return, as a token of love. The festival usually falls in August.

A sister ties a ribbon around her brother's arm at Rakhsha Bandhan.

Date Chart

Sikhs celebrate their festivals by the lunar calendar. Each month starts with a new moon and falls between our ordinary months.

Calendar Months	Sikh Festivals	
Magh (*Jan–Feb*)	*Maghi*	*Basant*
Phagan (*Feb–Mar*)	*Hola Mohalla*	
Chait (*Mar–Apr*)		
Vasakh (*Apr–May*)	*Baisakhi* (April 13)	
Jaith (*May–Jun*)	The martyrdom of Guru Arjan	
Har (*Jun–July*)	Birthday of Guru Har Krishan	
Sawan (*July–Aug*)		
Bhadro (*Aug–Sept*)	*Rakhsha Bandhan*	
Asun (*Sept–Oct*)	Installation of the Guru Granth Sahib	Birthday of Guru Ram Das
Katik (*Oct–Nov*)	*Diwali*	Birthday of Guru Nanak
Magar (*Nov–Dec*)	The martyrdom of Guru Tegh Badadur	
Poh (*Dec–Jan*)	Birthday of Guru Gobind Singh	*Lohri*

The Sikh Gurus

1. Guru Nanak (1469–1539)
2. Guru Angad (1504–1552)
3. Guru Amar Das (1479–1574)
4. Guru Ram Das (1534–1581)
5. Guru Arjan (1563–1606)
6. Guru Hargobind (1595–1644)
7. Guru Har Rai (1630–1661)
8. Guru Har Krishan (1656–1664)
9. Guru Tegh Bahadur (1621–1675)
10. Guru Gobind Singh (1666–1708)

Glossary

Amrit Baptismal water

Caste A hereditary class into which a Hindu is born, denoting social status.

Chapatties Round, flat unleavened bread resembling a pancake.

Granthi A reader. He looks after the Guru Granth Sahib.

Gurdwara A Sikh place of worship. The word means "House of God."

Guru Granth Sahib The Sikh Holy Book, which contains 5,894 hymns and verses. It is written in *Gurmukhi* script.

Gurmukhi The written script of the Punjabi language. The word means "from the mouth of the Guru." It is the original script used for the sacred writings of the Sikhs.

Gurpurb A festival associated with a Guru.

Guru A religious teacher. When Sikhs speak of the Gurus, they usually mean the ten prophets on whose teachings their religion is based.

Khalsa Baptized Sikhs. The word means "pure ones." The first *Khalsa* were baptized by Guru Gobind Singh.

Kirtan The community singing of hymns to musical accompaniment.

Langar The name for the kitchen and the food that is prepared and eaten at the *gurdwara* after a service. It symbolizes unity and equality among Sikhs.

Mela A word meaning "fair," used to describe festivals other than *gurpurbs*.

Mogul A member of the Muslim dynasty of Indian emperors who ruled India from 1526.

Muslim A follower of the religion of Islam.

Panj Pyare "The five beloved Sikhs" who were the first *Khalsa*. Today the word is used for a group of five baptized Sikhs who perform baptisms at the *gurdwara*.

Prophet A person who speaks by inspiration from God; a person who predicts the future.

Turban A man's headdress, made by winding a long length of fabric around the head.

Further Reading

If you would like to find out more about Sikhs, you may like to read the following books:

A Sikh Wedding by Olivia Bennett (Hamish Hamilton, 1985)

I Am a Sikh by Manju Aggarwal (Watts, 1985)

The Sikh World by Daljit Singh (Silver Burdett, 1985)

Way of the Sikh (Dufour)

Index

Acknowledgments

The publisher would like to thank those who provided pictures on the following pages: Camerapix Hutchinson front cover, 9 (above), 12, 13, 17; S. Kapoor 44; Ann and Bury Peerless 5, 10, 16, 18, 19, 21, 22, 24, 28, 29, (above), 30, 43; David Richardson 4, 6, 7, 8, 11, 15, 20, 23, 25, 26, 27, 31, 32, 34, 35, 36, 37, 38, 39, 40, 41, 42; Wayland Picture Library 14, 33.

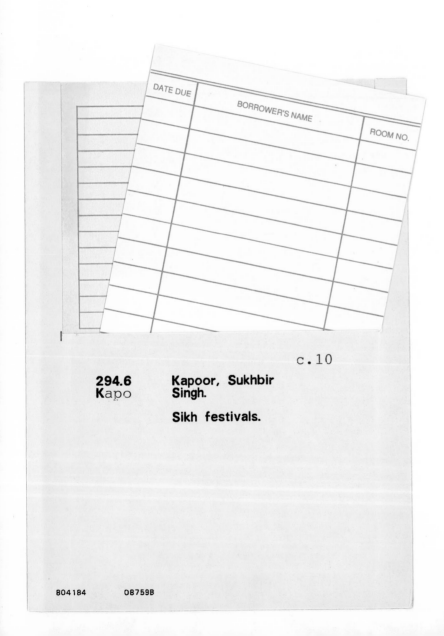

DATE DUE	BORROWER'S NAME	ROOM NO.

c.10

294.6   **Kapoor, Sukhbir**
Kapo   **Singh.**

            Sikh festivals.